HAITI

a coloring book for grown ups

∧ Light Messages

Haiti: A Coloring Book for Grown Ups
www.lightmessages.com
books@lightmessages.com

Images by Richar

Published 2016, by Light Messages
www.lightmessages.com
Durham, NC 27713 USA
SAN: 920-9298

ISBN: 978-1-61153-232-6

ARTWORK
The images of this book were hand-drawn by the artist Richar, who specializes in fine art pen and ink drawings. To contact Richar or inquire about his other artwork, please email books@lightmessages.com.

Catalog of images in order of appearance: Man and woman carrying baskets; Drum; Banana patch; Tropical fish; Fishermen; Vodou symbol for Erzuli; *Neg Mawon* statue; Cow; Christmas paper lanterns; Collection of traditional baskets; Vendor (*Machann*); Traditional gingerbread house; Oxen; Flamingoes; Hibiscus; Market Scene; Mountains; Tap-Tap; Washing clothes; Sugarcane; Neighborhood of Jalousie, Petionville; Caiman; Drums; Goat; Iron Market facade; Iron Market scene; Pigs; Parrots; King Henri Christophe's Sans-Souci Palace in Milo; Fishing boats; Mabouya; Paper kites

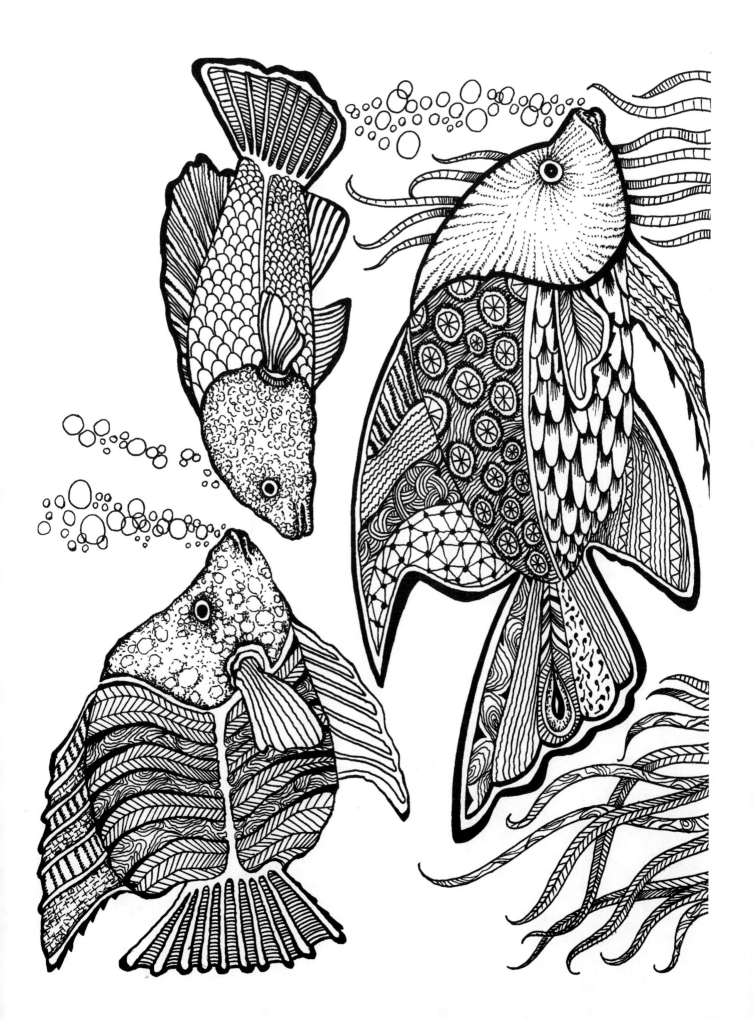

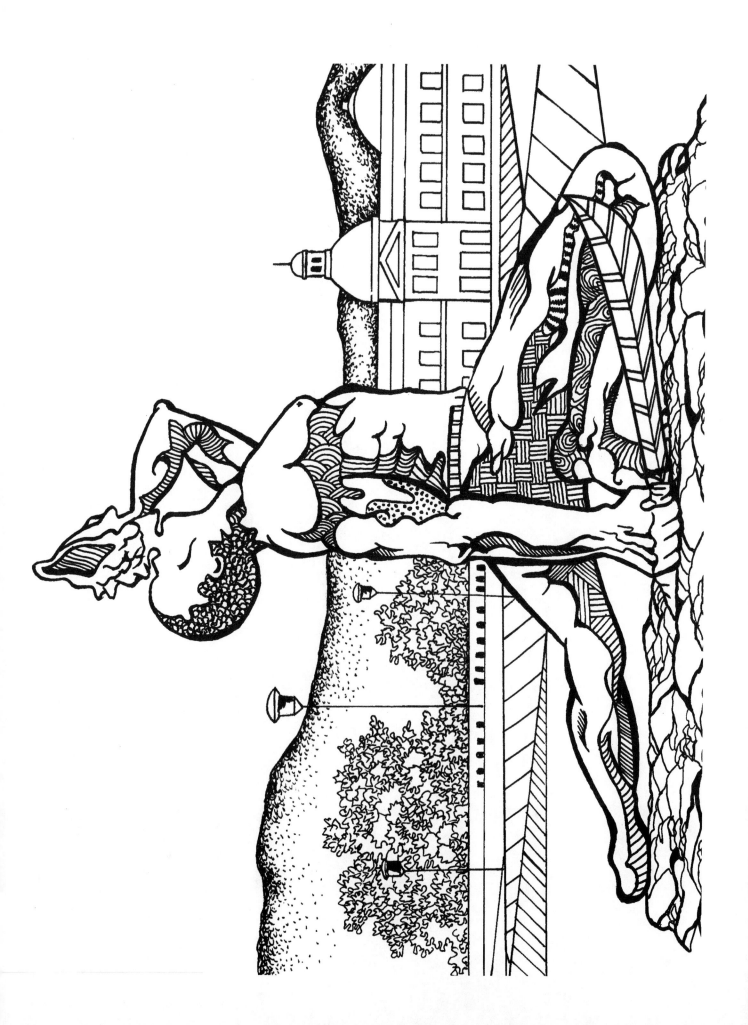

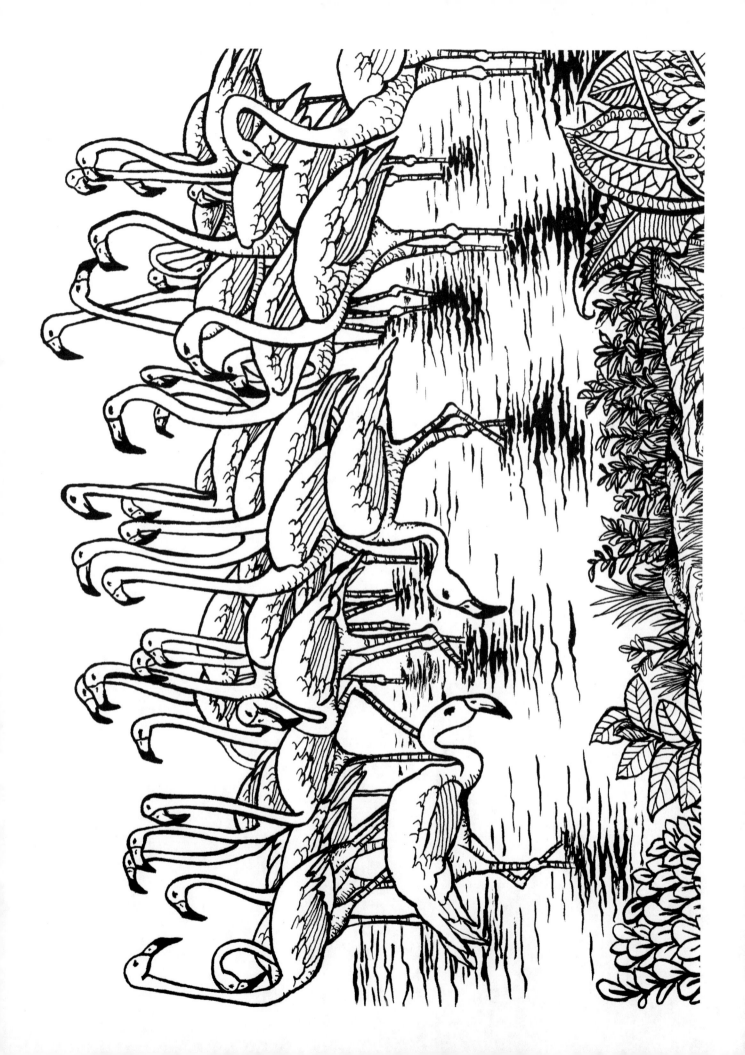

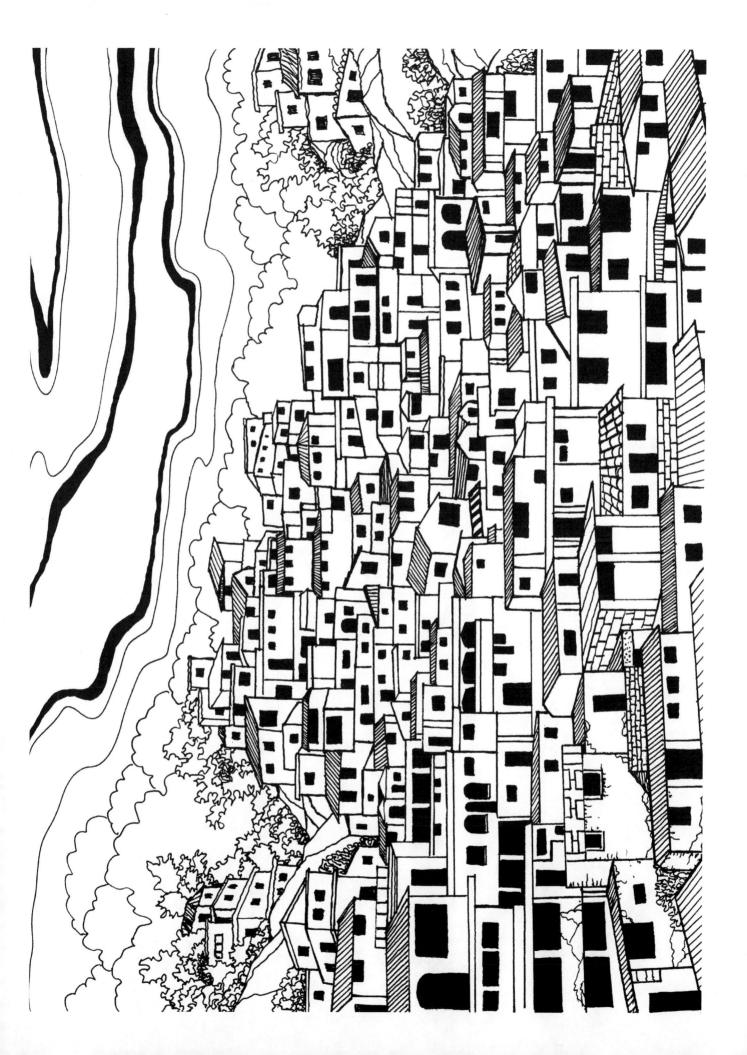

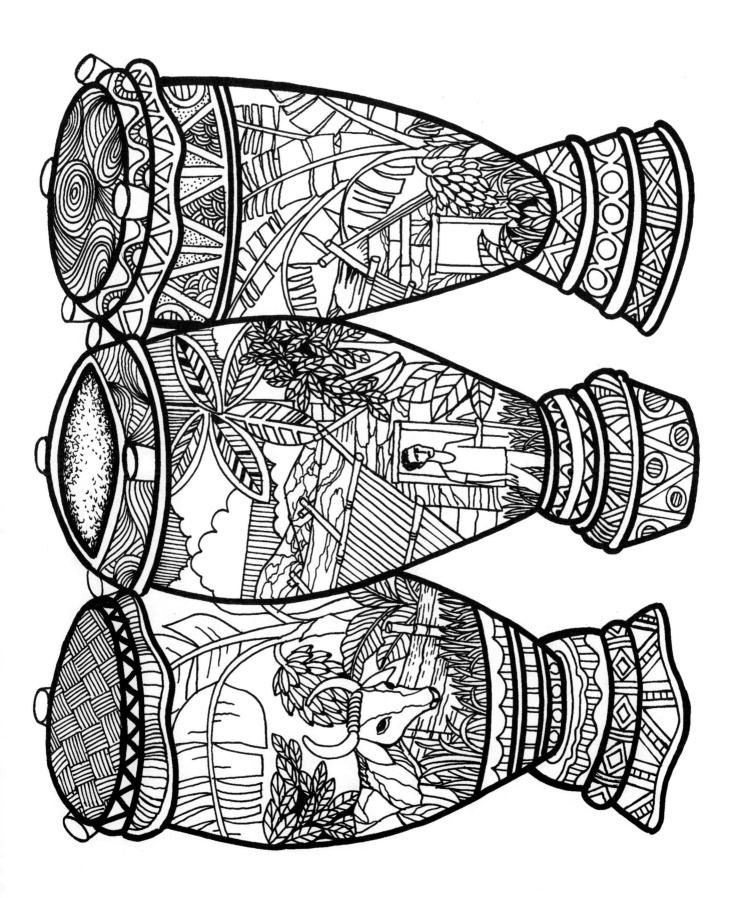

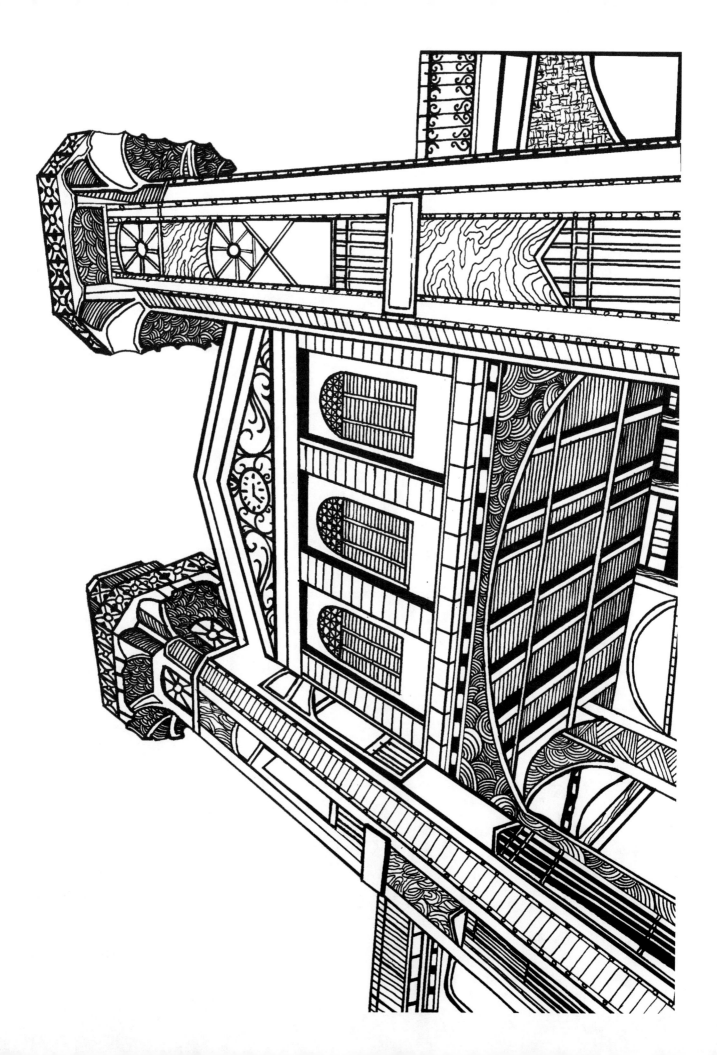

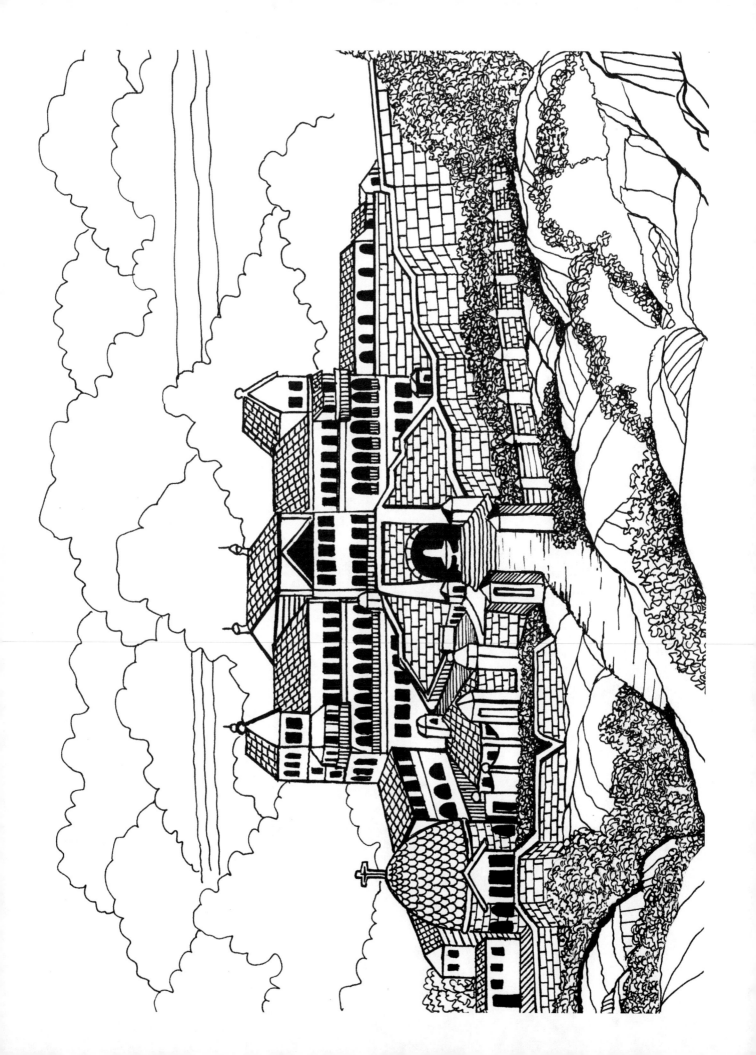

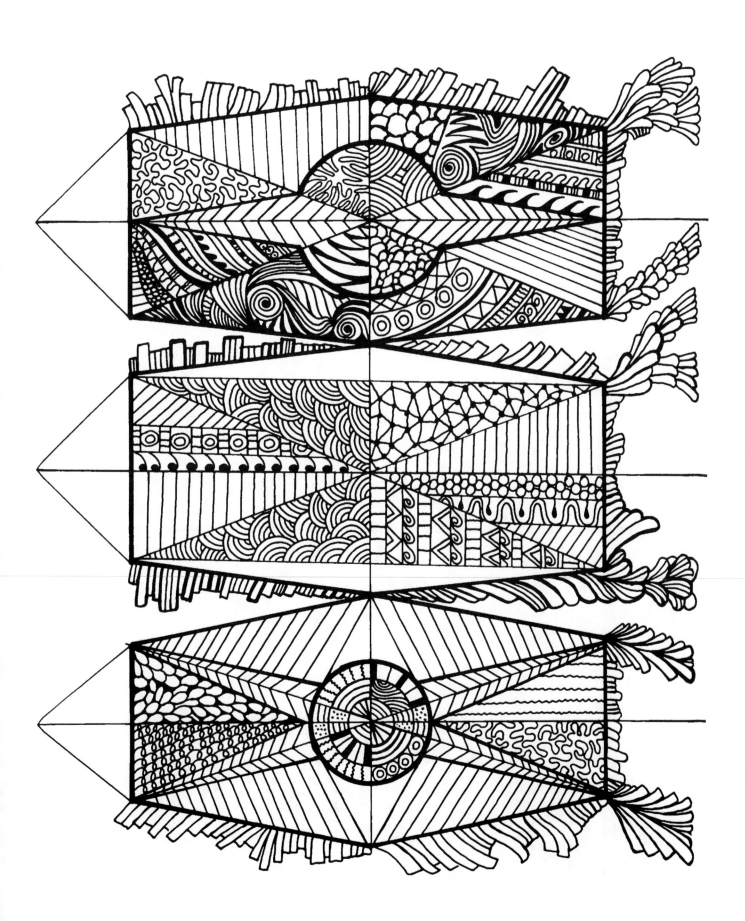

EXPLORE HAITI
WITH THESE TITLES

JANJAK AND FREDA GO TO THE IRON MARKET
Written by Elizabeth Turnbull; Illustrated by Mark Jones; Creole text by Wally Turnbull
In this first book of the bilingual Janjak and Freda series, cousins Janjak and Freda go with their godmother on an exciting adventure to Haiti's famous Iron Market. While there, they make many new friends, taste new fruits, and show the value of helping others when a runaway goat causes havoc in the market. The colorful text and beautiful illustrations will leave children dreaming up their own adventures.

BONNWIT KABRIT
Written by Elizabeth Turnbull; Illustrated by Erin Vaganos
"Well worth acquiring." –*Kirkus Reviews*. In this delightful, rhyming bedtime story, children journey across Haiti, saying goodnight to scenes the nation's children would know from their daily lives. From the calico cat to the pink flowers of the bouganvillea to the sweet goat nestled beneath the starry sky, children will embark on an exciting bedtime journey as one by one they say, *bonnwit*.

BEL PEYI MWEN
Text by Elizabeth Turnbull; Illustrated by Kris Battles
This coloring book for children takes young artists on a journey through typical scenes of Haiti, with short paragraphs of text to help them learn about the country and her people.

HIDDEN MEANINGS: TRUTH AND SECRET IN HAITI'S CREOLE PROVERBS
By Wally Turnbull
A collection of the colorful proverbs that characterize the country of Haiti and its people. The proverbs appear in the original Creole with accompanying translations. Whenever possible, literal rather than common translations are provided that the reader may hear the language as well as the proverbs. Also included are explanations of the proverbs' meanings. Featuring over 1200 entries, this is, to date, the most varied, complete, and accurate collection of Haitian proverbs.

CREOLE MADE EASY
By Wally Turnbull
The best-selling, simple introduction to Haitian Creole for English speaking people. Sixteen easy lessons cover the basic elements of Creole grammar and how to pronounce Creole words. The lessons include simple exercises and translation keys. A thorough up to date dictionary of over 4,600 Creole to English and English to Creole word translations is included. Over 100,000 copies sold!

Printed in the USA
CPSIA information can be obtained
at www.ICGtesting.com
LVHW061539230823
755929LV00013B/378

9 781611 532326

WINNER OF:

Midwest Book Award

Benjamin Franklin Award

Moonbeam Children's
Book Award

47 Strings
Tessa's Special Code

Written by Becky Carey • Illustrated by Bonnie Leick

LITTLE CREEK PRESS®
AND BOOK DESIGN

Mineral Point, Wisconsin USA

Little Creek Press®
A Division of Kristin Mitchell Design, Inc.
5341 Sunny Ridge Road
Mineral Point, Wisconsin 53565

Illustrator: Bonnie Leick
Editor: Carrie Stidwell O'Boyle
Book Design and Project Coordination: Little Creek Press

Seventh Printing
October 2021

Printed in United States of America.

For more information or to order books:
www.littlecreekpress.com

Library of Congress Control Number: 2012950955

ISBN-13: 978-1-942586-07-4

Dedication:

Tessa — may you always follow your heart,
dream bigger than life, and achieve unlimited greatness.

Casin — for showing me how to see the world through the eyes of a child.
~ Becky Carey

For Zepplin and Zoe
~ B.L.

Acknowledgments:

When we embarked on this adventure, I had no idea a little family video we created to explain baby Tessa's Down syndrome diagnosis to her brother, Casin, would not only be discovered by thousands of people on YouTube, but also by Little Creek Press who brought our story to life via this book. Thank you to everyone who believed that what I had to say was worth something, for validating my passion for a cause and for supporting me in this humbling endeavor.

Thank you to all of our family and friends for their unwavering support that holds a special place in my heart. To my sister Erika who played a large role in the development of *47 Strings*. I am truly grateful for the help and guidance that helped land me here today. With great sisterly love, thank you.

Thank you is certainly not enough for my husband, Dan, whose gracious encouragement has never gone unnoticed. My biggest enthusiast, as well as Tessa's, he never misses an opportunity to say how proud he is of his family. I will be forever grateful to have Dan in my life — probably more than he will ever know.

Finally, to my daughters Tessa, Kendal, son Dax, and my stepson Casin: Without you, this story would not exist. Your little lives have touched countless others' in a big way just because you are yourselves: such charming, affectionate and precocious little beings. You bring us so much joy. We are above and beyond privileged to be your parents.

Dear Reader:

I was inspired to write this book by the birth of our beautiful daughter, Tessa, who was born with 47 chromosomes instead of the typical 46 — also known as Down syndrome. I wanted to explain to our 7-year-old son, Casin, his sister's diagnosis in a way that was relaxed, understandable and heartfelt. This book is a love letter to our children and I hope it helps express our belief that we can all celebrate our differences — whatever they may be — and love unconditionally.

Warmly,
Becky Carey

Dear Casin:

Do you remember when your
little sister Tessa was born?

Do you remember how much she made you smile?

She was so little and sweet, and she
LOVED to cuddle with you!

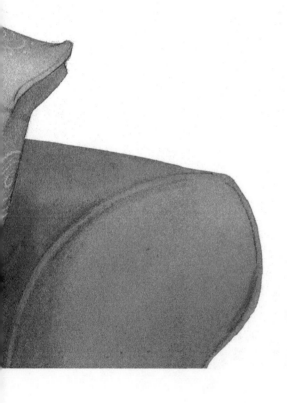

We know a lot of things about Tessa:

She has big blue eyes...
soft smushy cheeks...
long pretty hair...
and a big, happy smile!

But there is one thing about
Tessa you don't know:

Tessa was born with Down syndrome.

What is Down syndrome?

All of our bodies are made from a special code.
This code is made of long strings that join together
to create the person we are when we are born.

Our special codes make us all learn, think, talk, move and look differently.

You have 46 strings
in your special code.

Tessa has 1 extra string
in her special code —
she has 47 strings.

All people with Down syndrome have 47 strings
in their special code. This just means that...

Sometimes, it might take Tessa a little
more time to learn new things.

Some of her muscles are a little weaker,
so she needs extra help and exercises
to make them stronger.

She might not be able to do some of the same
things at the same time as other kids her age.

She will look a little different than you and me.

But most importantly it means...

We have a little bit more of her to love!

Tessa will always have Down syndrome.

It will be a part of her for her whole life.

Some people might not understand what it means to have Down syndrome or think it's a bad thing. They might pick on Tessa, or treat her differently.

That's why Tessa needs her friends and family to be there for her... to protect her, and to teach people that it is okay to be her friend... and to love her, just like we do!

As she grows up, Tessa will
do lots of cool things like...

Ride a bike...

Fly a kite...

Go to school...

Have lots of fun...

and SO many other
exciting things...
just like you!

Tessa will always have a lot of important
people in her life, and we are glad
that you are one of them!

Your special codes might be different,
but we love you BOTH the same.

Love,
Your Parents

The End

About the Author: Becky Carey

Writer and mom Becky Carey exposes her life raising her daughter Tessa, who has Down syndrome, on her blog, Dear Tessa (visit at www.deartessa.com). An advocate for her daughter and others with "47 strings," Becky strives to change the outdated stereotypes of Down syndrome. Becky, her husband Dan, and their children reside in southwest Wisconsin.

This book has become more than a tool for educating children on how to accept difference. It has become a launching pad for families to move forward together after a diagnosis presents itself.

Little Britches Photography

About the Artist: Bonnie Leick

Bonnie Leick (*like*) grew up on a dairy farm in Central Wisconsin where, as a child, she spent her summers picking rocks in the fields and baling hay. Bonnie's award-winning artwork has sometimes been defined as quirky and humorous. Although she paints with watercolors, many think that her artwork is done digitally. That does not mean that she hasn't used the computer. Bonnie has worked for publishers such as Simon & Schuster, Two Lions and Random House. She has also illustrated for *Highlights High Five* and *Highlights*. Before her work in children's books, Bonnie received a BFA in Film/Video-Character Animation from the California Institute of Art and Design. She worked in the animation industry until switching her career to become a children's book illustrator. Bonnie currently resides in Jackson, Wisconsin, with her husband Douglas O'Leary. She has two stepsons, Ryan and Connor, and two French Bulldogs, Zoe and Zepplin. To view more of Bonnie's artwork, please visit her website at www.bonnieleick.com.

About Down Syndrome

Down syndrome is the most common genetic disorder. It occurs in approximately 1/800 births in the United States. The cause of Down syndrome is a difference in the amount of chromosome material — namely chromosome 21.

In most people, each cell has 46 chromosomes that are arranged in 23 pairs. The chromosome pairs are numbered 1-22 based on size. The 23rd pair of chromosomes determines the individual's sex. At conception, the fetus receives 23 chromosomes from his/her mother and 23 from his/her father for the total of 46 chromosomes.

Individuals with Down syndrome have extra genetic material from chromosome 21. Most commonly, individuals have a third copy of chromosome 21 (called trisomy 21). Trisomy 21 is caused by the nondisjunction (not breaking apart) of the pair chromosome 21 in an egg or sperm cell leading to the extra chromosome 21.

The extra material from chromosome 21 leads to the clinical features of Down syndrome. The physical features and medical issues associated with Down syndrome vary widely from person to person. Individuals with Down syndrome may have distinct physical features which are often recognizable, such as a flat facial profile, an upward slant to the eyes, small ears, and shorter pinky fingers. Down syndrome can also be associated with birth defects such as congenital heart disease and digestive system abnormalities. Individuals with Down syndrome tend to have low muscle tone, delayed physical and intellectual development and intellectual disability, and may have other medical issues such as low thyroid hormone, small size, chronic ear infections, and obstructive sleep apnea. Physical, occupational and speech therapy, as well as early-childhood education, can also help encourage and accelerate development.

Just like you and me, each child with Down syndrome is unique.

Jess Scott Schwoerer M.D.
Jody Haun MS, CGC
Down Syndrome Clinic
Waisman Center
The University of Wisconsin, Madison

About Down Syndrome Diagnosis Network

Down Syndrome Diagnosis Network (DSDN) launched in 2014 with a mission to inform, connect and support new families with a Down syndrome diagnosis. DSDN currently serves over 9,000 families in our small, private, online communities which focus on parents in the prenatal through age three stages. The DSDN Rockin' Mom and Rockin' Dad online birth clubs capture about 15% of all families with a new diagnosis each year. Through its Rockin' Family Fund, DSDN supports families with welcome gifts, scholarships to attend Down syndrome related events, care gifts for families experiencing long hospital stays and memorial gifts for those who lose a child. Each year, DSDN holds their Rockin' Mom Retreat to provide moms an opportunity to connect with other moms, be inspired and recharge.

In addition to supporting families, DSDN partners with medical providers and local Down syndrome organizations to provide them with information and resources to ensure all families have up-to-date information and access to support and connections after the diagnosis.

Down Syndrome Diagnosis Network's mission is to provide connections, support and accurate information to families with a new Down syndrome diagnosis. The DSDN vision is that all families would have diagnosis experiences that are unbiased and supported with current resources and information, every time, through which they quickly know they're not alone.

Learn more at: www.dsdiagnosisnetwork.org

DOWN SYNDROME DIAGNOSIS NETWORK

The DSDN was like having a support group, a flotation device and a hotline all wrapped into one! The groups are a constant reminder that everything is going to be okay and we weren't going to drown, even when everyone else led us to believe otherwise.

~Alexa Byrnes

DSDN got my full attention as I noticed how they included moms and welcomed everyone with such warm hearts. I felt so alone and had no clue on what I was doing as to raising a baby with down syndrome. DSDN is such a positive organization that has helped me along the way; I no longer feel alone, nor did I feel left out. I went on my first DSDN Rockin' Mom Retreat and it felt good to be around other moms who get it and to be so loved and supported by these wonderful moms all because of such an amazing organization – the DSDN!

~Jetter Freeman

Permission granted by Lara Segrest

Finding DSDN helped me to not feel alone right after our prenatal diagnosis. I hadn't shared the diagnosis with anyone besides my immediate family, so I didn't really feel like there was anyone I could talk to that would really understand how I was feeling and what I was thinking. After being connected to the group by another patient from my OB's office who had a one-year-old with DS, I had a place I could share my challenges, successes and questions. It made a huge difference in how I was feeling and how I feel now.

~Amy Hawrylo

After our birth diagnosis, I spiraled into a deep state of depression and anxiety. I stumbled onto the DSDN website and was immediately connected with other parents in similar situations. The DSDN truly helped me see how amazing this journey could be and inspired me to be a better therapist, advocate and an overall better mom.

~Sunnie Escota-Reyna

Permission granted by Heather Kamia

Permission granted by Monica Leon

Organizations and Support

A portion of the proceeds from this book will continue to benefit organizations like the Down Syndrome Diagnosis Network so that these great organizations can continue to ensure that all individuals with Down syndrome, and their families, have the opportunity to achieve their potential in all aspects of community life, while advancing awareness, respect and opportunity.

"We know that there will always be moments like this... where chromosomes don't matter and family does... moments like these when different doesn't equal less."

~ Becky Carey

THANK YOU

Printed in the USA
CPSIA information can be obtained
at www.ICGtesting.com
LVHW061539230823
755929LV00013B/379

9 781942 586074

WINNER OF:

Midwest Book Award

Benjamin Franklin Award

Moonbeam Children's
Book Award

47 Strings
Tessa's Special Code

Written by Becky Carey • Illustrated by Bonnie Leick

LITTLE CREEK PRESS
AND BOOK DESIGN

Mineral Point, Wisconsin USA

Little Creek Press®
A Division of Kristin Mitchell Design, Inc.
5341 Sunny Ridge Road
Mineral Point, Wisconsin 53565

Illustrator: Bonnie Leick
Editor: Carrie Stidwell O'Boyle
Book Design and Project Coordination: Little Creek Press

Seventh Printing
October 2021

Printed in United States of America.

For more information or to order books:
www.littlecreekpress.com

Library of Congress Control Number: 2012950955

ISBN-13: 978-1-942586-07-4

Dedication:

Tessa — may you always follow your heart,
dream bigger than life, and achieve unlimited greatness.

Casin — for showing me how to see the world through the eyes of a child.
~ Becky Carey

For Zepplin and Zoe
~ B.L.

Acknowledgments:

When we embarked on this adventure, I had no idea a little family video we created to explain baby Tessa's Down syndrome diagnosis to her brother, Casin, would not only be discovered by thousands of people on YouTube, but also by Little Creek Press who brought our story to life via this book. Thank you to everyone who believed that what I had to say was worth something, for validating my passion for a cause and for supporting me in this humbling endeavor.

Thank you to all of our family and friends for their unwavering support that holds a special place in my heart. To my sister Erika who played a large role in the development of *47 Strings*. I am truly grateful for the help and guidance that helped land me here today. With great sisterly love, thank you.

Thank you is certainly not enough for my husband, Dan, whose gracious encouragement has never gone unnoticed. My biggest enthusiast, as well as Tessa's, he never misses an opportunity to say how proud he is of his family. I will be forever grateful to have Dan in my life — probably more than he will ever know.

Finally, to my daughters Tessa, Kendal, son Dax, and my stepson Casin: Without you, this story would not exist. Your little lives have touched countless others' in a big way just because you are yourselves: such charming, affectionate and precocious little beings. You bring us so much joy. We are above and beyond privileged to be your parents.

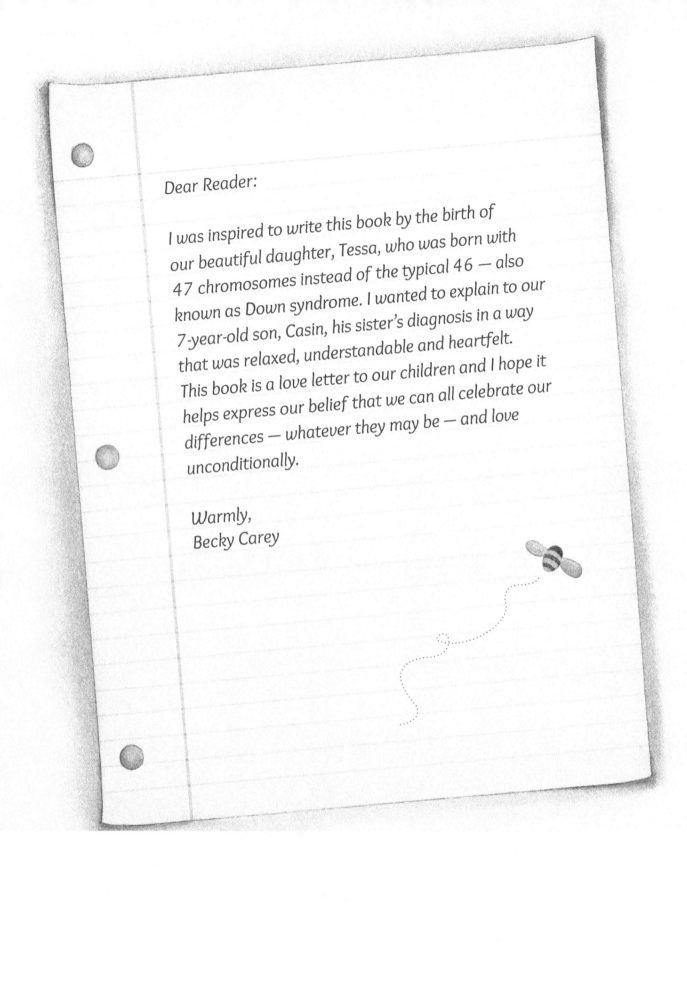

Dear Reader:

I was inspired to write this book by the birth of our beautiful daughter, Tessa, who was born with 47 chromosomes instead of the typical 46 — also known as Down syndrome. I wanted to explain to our 7-year-old son, Casin, his sister's diagnosis in a way that was relaxed, understandable and heartfelt. This book is a love letter to our children and I hope it helps express our belief that we can all celebrate our differences — whatever they may be — and love unconditionally.

Warmly,
Becky Carey

Dear Casin:

Do you remember when your
little sister Tessa was born?

Do you remember how much she made you smile?

She was so little and sweet, and she
LOVED to cuddle with you!

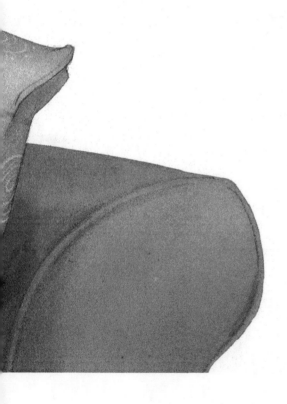

We know a lot of things about Tessa:

She has big blue eyes...
soft smushy cheeks...
long pretty hair...
and a big, happy smile!

But there is one thing about
Tessa you don't know:

Tessa was born with Down syndrome.

What is Down syndrome?

All of our bodies are made from a special code.
This code is made of long strings that join together
to create the person we are when we are born.

Our special codes make us all learn, think,
talk, move and look differently.

You have 46 strings
in your special code.

Tessa has 1 extra string
in her special code —
she has 47 strings.

All people with Down syndrome have 47 strings in their special code. This just means that...

Sometimes, it might take Tessa a little
more time to learn new things.

Some of her muscles are a little weaker,
so she needs extra help and exercises
to make them stronger.

She might not be able to do some of the same
things at the same time as other kids her age.

She will look a little different than you and me.

But most importantly it means...

We have a little bit more of her to love!

Tessa will always have Down syndrome.

It will be a part of her for her whole life.

Some people might not understand what it means to have Down syndrome or think it's a bad thing. They might pick on Tessa, or treat her differently.

That's why Tessa needs her friends and family to be there for her... to protect her, and to teach people that it is okay to be her friend... and to love her, just like we do!

As she grows up, Tessa will
do lots of cool things like...

Ride a bike...

Fly a kite...

Go to school...

Have lots of fun...

and SO many other
exciting things...
just like you!

Tessa will always have a lot of important
people in her life, and we are glad
that you are one of them!

Your special codes might be different,
but we love you BOTH the same.

Love,
Your Parents

The End

About the Author: Becky Carey

*W*riter and mom Becky Carey exposes her life raising her daughter Tessa, who has Down syndrome, on her blog, Dear Tessa (visit at www.deartessa.com). An advocate for her daughter and others with "47 strings," Becky strives to change the outdated stereotypes of Down syndrome. Becky, her husband Dan, and their children reside in southwest Wisconsin.

This book has become more than a tool for educating children on how to accept difference. It has become a launching pad for families to move forward together after a diagnosis presents itself.

Little Britches Photography

About the Artist: Bonnie Leick

Bonnie Leick (*like*) grew up on a dairy farm in Central Wisconsin where, as a child, she spent her summers picking rocks in the fields and baling hay. Bonnie's award-winning artwork has sometimes been defined as quirky and humorous. Although she paints with watercolors, many think that her artwork is done digitally. That does not mean that she hasn't used the computer. Bonnie has worked for publishers such as Simon & Schuster, Two Lions and Random House. She has also illustrated for *Highlights High Five* and *Highlights*. Before her work in children's books, Bonnie received a BFA in Film/Video-Character Animation from the California Institute of Art and Design. She worked in the animation industry until switching her career to become a children's book illustrator. Bonnie currently resides in Jackson, Wisconsin, with her husband Douglas O'Leary. She has two stepsons, Ryan and Connor, and two French Bulldogs, Zoe and Zepplin. To view more of Bonnie's artwork, please visit her website at www.bonnieleick.com.

About Down Syndrome

Down syndrome is the most common genetic disorder. It occurs in approximately 1/800 births in the United States. The cause of Down syndrome is a difference in the amount of chromosome material — namely chromosome 21.

In most people, each cell has 46 chromosomes that are arranged in 23 pairs. The chromosome pairs are numbered 1-22 based on size. The 23rd pair of chromosomes determines the individual's sex. At conception, the fetus receives 23 chromosomes from his/her mother and 23 from his/her father for the total of 46 chromosomes.

Individuals with Down syndrome have extra genetic material from chromosome 21. Most commonly, individuals have a third copy of chromosome 21 (called trisomy 21). Trisomy 21 is caused by the nondisjunction (not breaking apart) of the pair chromosome 21 in an egg or sperm cell leading to the extra chromosome 21.

The extra material from chromosome 21 leads to the clinical features of Down syndrome. The physical features and medical issues associated with Down syndrome vary widely from person to person. Individuals with Down syndrome may have distinct physical features which are often recognizable, such as a flat facial profile, an upward slant to the eyes, small ears, and shorter pinky fingers. Down syndrome can also be associated with birth defects such as congenital heart disease and digestive system abnormalities. Individuals with Down syndrome tend to have low muscle tone, delayed physical and intellectual development and intellectual disability, and may have other medical issues such as low thyroid hormone, small size, chronic ear infections, and obstructive sleep apnea. Physical, occupational and speech therapy, as well as early-childhood education, can also help encourage and accelerate development.

Just like you and me, each child with Down syndrome is unique.

Jess Scott Schwoerer M.D.
Jody Haun MS, CGC
Down Syndrome Clinic
Waisman Center
The University of Wisconsin, Madison

About Down Syndrome Diagnosis Network

Down Syndrome Diagnosis Network (DSDN) launched in 2014 with a mission to inform, connect and support new families with a Down syndrome diagnosis. DSDN currently serves over 9,000 families in our small, private, online communities which focus on parents in the prenatal through age three stages. The DSDN Rockin' Mom and Rockin' Dad online birth clubs capture about 15% of all families with a new diagnosis each year. Through its Rockin' Family Fund, DSDN supports families with welcome gifts, scholarships to attend Down syndrome related events, care gifts for families experiencing long hospital stays and memorial gifts for those who lose a child. Each year, DSDN holds their Rockin' Mom Retreat to provide moms an opportunity to connect with other moms, be inspired and recharge.

In addition to supporting families, DSDN partners with medical providers and local Down syndrome organizations to provide them with information and resources to ensure all families have up-to-date information and access to support and connections after the diagnosis.

Down Syndrome Diagnosis Network's mission is to provide connections, support and accurate information to families with a new Down syndrome diagnosis. The DSDN vision is that all families would have diagnosis experiences that are unbiased and supported with current resources and information, every time, through which they quickly know they're not alone.

Learn more at: www.dsdiagnosisnetwork.org

DOWN SYNDROME DIAGNOSIS NETWORK

The DSDN was like having a support group, a flotation device and a hotline all wrapped into one! The groups are a constant reminder that everything is going to be okay and we weren't going to drown, even when everyone else led us to believe otherwise.
~Alexa Byrnes

DSDN got my full attention as I noticed how they included moms and welcomed everyone with such warm hearts. I felt so alone and had no clue on what I was doing as to raising a baby with down syndrome. DSDN is such a positive organization that has helped me along the way; I no longer feel alone, nor did I feel left out. I went on my first DSDN Rockin' Mom Retreat and it felt good to be around other moms who get it and to be so loved and supported by these wonderful moms all because of such an amazing organization – the DSDN!
~Jetter Freeman

Permission granted by Lara Segrest

Finding DSDN helped me to not feel alone right after our prenatal diagnosis. I hadn't shared the diagnosis with anyone besides my immediate family, so I didn't really feel like there was anyone I could talk to that would really understand how I was feeling and what I was thinking. After being connected to the group by another patient from my OB's office who had a one-year-old with DS, I had a place I could share my challenges, successes and questions. It made a huge difference in how I was feeling and how I feel now.

~Amy Hawrylo

After our birth diagnosis, I spiraled into a deep state of depression and anxiety. I stumbled onto the DSDN website and was immediately connected with other parents in similar situations. The DSDN truly helped me see how amazing this journey could be and inspired me to be a better therapist, advocate and an overall better mom.

~Sunnie Escota-Reyna

Permission granted by Heather Kamia

Permission granted by Monica Leon

Organizations and Support

A portion of the proceeds from this book will continue to benefit organizations like the Down Syndrome Diagnosis Network so that these great organizations can continue to ensure that all individuals with Down syndrome, and their families, have the opportunity to achieve their potential in all aspects of community life, while advancing awareness, respect and opportunity.

"We know that there will always be moments like this... where chromosomes don't matter and family does... moments like these when different doesn't equal less."

~ Becky Carey

THANK YOU

Printed in the USA
CPSIA information can be obtained
at www.ICGtesting.com
LVHW061539230823
755929LV00013B/379

9 781942 586074

WINNER OF:

Midwest Book Award

Benjamin Franklin Award

Moonbeam Children's
Book Award

47 Strings
Tessa's Special Code

Written by Becky Carey • Illustrated by Bonnie Leick

LITTLE CREEK PRESS®
AND BOOK DESIGN

Mineral Point, Wisconsin USA

Little Creek Press®
A Division of Kristin Mitchell Design, Inc.
5341 Sunny Ridge Road
Mineral Point, Wisconsin 53565

Illustrator: Bonnie Leick
Editor: Carrie Stidwell O'Boyle
Book Design and Project Coordination: Little Creek Press

Seventh Printing
October 2021

Printed in United States of America.

For more information or to order books:
www.littlecreekpress.com

Library of Congress Control Number: 2012950955

ISBN-13: 978-1-942586-07-4

Dedication:

Tessa — may you always follow your heart,
dream bigger than life, and achieve unlimited greatness.

Casin — for showing me how to see the world through the eyes of a child.
~ Becky Carey

For Zepplin and Zoe
~ B.L.

Acknowledgments:

When we embarked on this adventure, I had no idea a little family video we created to explain baby Tessa's Down syndrome diagnosis to her brother, Casin, would not only be discovered by thousands of people on YouTube, but also by Little Creek Press who brought our story to life via this book. Thank you to everyone who believed that what I had to say was worth something, for validating my passion for a cause and for supporting me in this humbling endeavor.

Thank you to all of our family and friends for their unwavering support that holds a special place in my heart. To my sister Erika who played a large role in the development of *47 Strings*. I am truly grateful for the help and guidance that helped land me here today. With great sisterly love, thank you.

Thank you is certainly not enough for my husband, Dan, whose gracious encouragement has never gone unnoticed. My biggest enthusiast, as well as Tessa's, he never misses an opportunity to say how proud he is of his family. I will be forever grateful to have Dan in my life — probably more than he will ever know.

Finally, to my daughters Tessa, Kendal, son Dax, and my stepson Casin: Without you, this story would not exist. Your little lives have touched countless others' in a big way just because you are yourselves: such charming, affectionate and precocious little beings. You bring us so much joy. We are above and beyond privileged to be your parents.

Dear Reader:

I was inspired to write this book by the birth of our beautiful daughter, Tessa, who was born with 47 chromosomes instead of the typical 46 — also known as Down syndrome. I wanted to explain to our 7-year-old son, Casin, his sister's diagnosis in a way that was relaxed, understandable and heartfelt. This book is a love letter to our children and I hope it helps express our belief that we can all celebrate our differences — whatever they may be — and love unconditionally.

Warmly,
Becky Carey

Dear Casin:

Do you remember when your
little sister Tessa was born?

Do you remember how much she made you smile?

She was so little and sweet, and she
LOVED to cuddle with you!

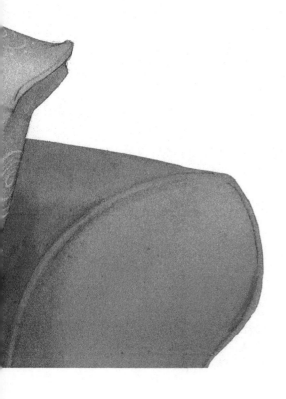

We know a lot of things about Tessa:

She has big blue eyes...
soft smushy cheeks...
long pretty hair...
and a big, happy smile!

But there is one thing about
Tessa you don't know:

Tessa was born with Down syndrome.

What is Down syndrome?

All of our bodies are made from a special code.
This code is made of long strings that join together
to create the person we are when we are born.

Our special codes make us all learn, think,
talk, move and look differently.

You have 46 strings
in your special code.

Tessa has 1 extra string
in her special code —
she has 47 strings.

All people with Down syndrome have 47 strings
in their special code. This just means that...

Sometimes, it might take Tessa a little
more time to learn new things.

Some of her muscles are a little weaker,
so she needs extra help and exercises
to make them stronger.

She might not be able to do some of the same
things at the same time as other kids her age.

She will look a little different than you and me.

But most importantly it means...

We have a little bit more of her to love!

Tessa will always have Down syndrome.

It will be a part of her for her whole life.

Some people might not understand what it means to have Down syndrome or think it's a bad thing. They might pick on Tessa, or treat her differently.

That's why Tessa needs her friends and family to be there for her... to protect her, and to teach people that it is okay to be her friend... and to love her, just like we do!

As she grows up, Tessa will
do lots of cool things like...

Ride a bike...

Fly a kite...

Go to school...

Have lots of fun...

and SO many other
exciting things...
just like you!

Tessa will always have a lot of important
people in her life, and we are glad
that you are one of them!

Your special codes might be different,
but we love you BOTH the same.

Love,
Your Parents

The End

About the Author: Becky Carey

W riter and mom Becky Carey exposes her life raising her daughter Tessa, who has Down syndrome, on her blog, Dear Tessa (visit at www.deartessa.com). An advocate for her daughter and others with "47 strings," Becky strives to change the outdated stereotypes of Down syndrome. Becky, her husband Dan, and their children reside in southwest Wisconsin.

This book has become more than a tool for educating children on how to accept difference. It has become a launching pad for families to move forward together after a diagnosis presents itself.

Little Britches Photography

About the Artist: Bonnie Leick

Bonnie Leick (*like*) grew up on a dairy farm in Central Wisconsin where, as a child, she spent her summers picking rocks in the fields and baling hay. Bonnie's award-winning artwork has sometimes been defined as quirky and humorous. Although she paints with watercolors, many think that her artwork is done digitally. That does not mean that she hasn't used the computer. Bonnie has worked for publishers such as Simon & Schuster, Two Lions and Random House. She has also illustrated for *Highlights High Five* and *Highlights*. Before her work in children's books, Bonnie received a BFA in Film/Video-Character Animation from the California Institute of Art and Design. She worked in the animation industry until switching her career to become a children's book illustrator. Bonnie currently resides in Jackson, Wisconsin, with her husband Douglas O'Leary. She has two stepsons, Ryan and Connor, and two French Bulldogs, Zoe and Zepplin. To view more of Bonnie's artwork, please visit her website at www.bonnieleick.com.

About Down Syndrome

Down syndrome is the most common genetic disorder. It occurs in approximately 1/800 births in the United States. The cause of Down syndrome is a difference in the amount of chromosome material — namely chromosome 21.

In most people, each cell has 46 chromosomes that are arranged in 23 pairs. The chromosome pairs are numbered 1-22 based on size. The 23rd pair of chromosomes determines the individual's sex. At conception, the fetus receives 23 chromosomes from his/her mother and 23 from his/her father for the total of 46 chromosomes.

Individuals with Down syndrome have extra genetic material from chromosome 21. Most commonly, individuals have a third copy of chromosome 21 (called trisomy 21). Trisomy 21 is caused by the nondisjunction (not breaking apart) of the pair chromosome 21 in an egg or sperm cell leading to the extra chromosome 21.

The extra material from chromosome 21 leads to the clinical features of Down syndrome. The physical features and medical issues associated with Down syndrome vary widely from person to person. Individuals with Down syndrome may have distinct physical features which are often recognizable, such as a flat facial profile, an upward slant to the eyes, small ears, and shorter pinky fingers. Down syndrome can also be associated with birth defects such as congenital heart disease and digestive system abnormalities. Individuals with Down syndrome tend to have low muscle tone, delayed physical and intellectual development and intellectual disability, and may have other medical issues such as low thyroid hormone, small size, chronic ear infections, and obstructive sleep apnea. Physical, occupational and speech therapy, as well as early-childhood education, can also help encourage and accelerate development.

Just like you and me, each child with Down syndrome is unique.

Jess Scott Schwoerer M.D.
Jody Haun MS, CGC
Down Syndrome Clinic
Waisman Center
The University of Wisconsin, Madison

About Down Syndrome Diagnosis Network

Down Syndrome Diagnosis Network (DSDN) launched in 2014 with a mission to inform, connect and support new families with a Down syndrome diagnosis. DSDN currently serves over 9,000 families in our small, private, online communities which focus on parents in the prenatal through age three stages. The DSDN Rockin' Mom and Rockin' Dad online birth clubs capture about 15% of all families with a new diagnosis each year. Through its Rockin' Family Fund, DSDN supports families with welcome gifts, scholarships to attend Down syndrome related events, care gifts for families experiencing long hospital stays and memorial gifts for those who lose a child. Each year, DSDN holds their Rockin' Mom Retreat to provide moms an opportunity to connect with other moms, be inspired and recharge.

In addition to supporting families, DSDN partners with medical providers and local Down syndrome organizations to provide them with information and resources to ensure all families have up-to-date information and access to support and connections after the diagnosis.

Down Syndrome Diagnosis Network's mission is to provide connections, support and accurate information to families with a new Down syndrome diagnosis. The DSDN vision is that all families would have diagnosis experiences that are unbiased and supported with current resources and information, every time, through which they quickly know they're not alone.

Learn more at: www.dsdiagnosisnetwork.org

DOWN SYNDROME DIAGNOSIS NETWORK

The DSDN was like having a support group, a flotation device and a hotline all wrapped into one! The groups are a constant reminder that everything is going to be okay and we weren't going to drown, even when everyone else led us to believe otherwise.
~Alexa Byrnes

DSDN got my full attention as I noticed how they included moms and welcomed everyone with such warm hearts. I felt so alone and had no clue on what I was doing as to raising a baby with down syndrome. DSDN is such a positive organization that has helped me along the way; I no longer feel alone, nor did I feel left out. I went on my first DSDN Rockin' Mom Retreat and it felt good to be around other moms who get it and to be so loved and supported by these wonderful moms all because of such an amazing organization – the DSDN!
~Jetter Freeman

Permission granted by Lara Segrest

Finding DSDN helped me to not feel alone right after our prenatal diagnosis. I hadn't shared the diagnosis with anyone besides my immediate family, so I didn't really feel like there was anyone I could talk to that would really understand how I was feeling and what I was thinking. After being connected to the group by another patient from my OB's office who had a one-year-old with DS, I had a place I could share my challenges, successes and questions. It made a huge difference in how I was feeling and how I feel now.

~Amy Hawrylo

After our birth diagnosis, I spiraled into a deep state of depression and anxiety. I stumbled onto the DSDN website and was immediately connected with other parents in similar situations. The DSDN truly helped me see how amazing this journey could be and inspired me to be a better therapist, advocate and an overall better mom.

~Sunnie Escota-Reyna

Permission granted by Heather Kamia

Permission granted by Monica Leon

Organizations and Support

A portion of the proceeds from this book will continue to benefit organizations like the Down Syndrome Diagnosis Network so that these great organizations can continue to ensure that all individuals with Down syndrome, and their families, have the opportunity to achieve their potential in all aspects of community life, while advancing awareness, respect and opportunity.

"We know that there will always be moments like this... where chromosomes don't matter and family does... moments like these when different doesn't equal less."

~ Becky Carey

THANK YOU

—

Printed in the USA
CPSIA information can be obtained
at www.ICGtesting.com
LVHW061539230823
755929LV00013B/379

"Heroic" Polonaise No.6 in A-flat major

By

Frédéric Chopin

For Solo Piano

(1842)

Op.53

Read & Co.

Copyright © 2021 Read & Co. Books

This edition is published by Read & Co. Books,
an imprint of Read & Co.

This book is copyright and may not be reproduced or copied in any
way without the express permission of the publisher in writing.

British Library Cataloguing-in-Publication Data
A catalogue record for this book is available
from the British Library.

Read & Co. is part of Read Books Ltd.
For more information visit
www.readandcobooks.co.uk

Polonaise.

a Mr. A. LEO.

F. CHOPIN, Op. 53.

Printed in the USA
CPSIA information can be obtained
at www.ICGtesting.com
LVHW061540230823
755929LV00013B/380

9 781446 516126